Teacher of the Devas

The Buddha's Relationship with the Gods

Susan Elbaum Jootla

Buddhist Publication Society
Kandy • Sri Lanka

Published in 1997

Buddhist Publication Society
P.O. Box 61
54, Sangharaja Mawatha
Kandy, Sri Lanka

ISBN 955-24-0160-7

Typeset at the BPS

Printed in Sri Lanka by
Karunaratne & Sons Ltd.
647, Kularatne Mawatha
Colombo 10

THE WHEEL PUBLICATION NO. 414/416

Contents

To My Teachers,
My Parents, and
My Husband

Namo Tassa Bhagavato, Arahato, Sammā Sambuddhassa

I

Introduction

In the canonical formula for contemplation of the Buddha, nine epithets of the Awakened One are mentioned. One of these, likely to be overlooked, is *satthā devamanussānaṁ*, "teacher of gods and humans." The present essay focuses on one aspect of this epithet: the Buddha's role as teacher of the devas or gods. In the pages to follow we will carefully consider the instructions and techniques he used when teaching beings of divine stature. If we study these teachings we will gain deeper understanding of how we should purify our own minds, and by studying the responses of the gods we can find models for our own behaviour in relation to the Master and his teaching.

Many religious leaders consider themselves prophets whose authority stems from an Almighty God, but as our epithet implies, the Buddha's relationship to divinity was very different. He instructed deities, as well as humans, on how to end all suffering (*dukkha*) by eradicating ignorance and other unwholesome states. The gods came to the Buddha to request instruction and clarification, to support his Sāsana or Dispensation, to praise his incomparable qualities, and to pay homage at his feet. Devas and brahmās are often mentioned throughout the Pāli Canon. They regularly manifest themselves on the human plane and participate in many episodes of the Buddha's career. Some of these higher beings are foolish, some exceedingly wise; some are barely distinguishable from well-off people, others are extremely powerful, long-lived, and magnificent. The multiple connections between the Buddha and beings of the higher planes can inspire meditators to develop the Noble Eightfold Path that leads to the end of suffering.

This essay will explore: (1) the Buddha's direct instructions to devas and how they can help human meditators practise the Dhamma; (2) how devas, out of gratitude and faith, honour the Buddha and support his Dispensation; and (3) the process of attaining liberation for devas, brahmās, and humans.

The chart on the facing page shows the thirty-one planes of existence in the Buddhist picture of the universe. Every being lives on one or another of these planes. After death all beings, except the arahants, will be reborn in a realm and under circumstances that accords with their kamma—their volitional actions of body, speech, and mind made in that existence or in any previous one. We will often refer to this chart to indicate where, in the cosmic hierarchy, the deities we meet come from.

The lowest area (planes 1–11) is called the sensuous realm; here sense experience predominates. Next comes the fine-material realm (12–27) attained by practising the fine-material absorptions (*rūpa-jhānas*). Above that is the immaterial realm (28–31) attained by practising the immaterial absorptions (*arūpa-jhānas*).

Although humans appear to be rather low on the scale, many intelligent deities long for rebirth on the human plane. Why? Because the best opportunity to practise the Dhamma and attain liberation is right here on earth. On the lower four planes, little progress can be made as suffering is gross and unrelenting and the opportunity to perform deeds of merit is rarely gained. The very bliss of the higher planes beclouds the universal characteristics of all phenomena: impermanence, unsatisfactoriness, and the lack of any lasting, controlling self.

Thirty-One Planes of Existence

Four Planes of the Immaterial Brahmā Realm			(31) Plane of Neither Perception-nor-non-Perception (30) Plane of Nothingness (29) Plane of Infinite Consciousness (28) Plane of Infinite Space
Sixteen Planes of the Fine Material Brahmā Realm	7 Fourth Jhāna Planes	5 Pure Abodes (Non-Return-ers)	(27) Highest (Akaniṭṭhā) (26) Clear Sighted (Sudassī) (25) Beautiful (Sudassā) (24) Serene (Atappā) (23) Durable (Avihā)
			(22) Non-percipient, matter only, no mind (21) Great Fruit
	3 Third Jhāna Planes		(20) Third Jhāna, highest degree (19) Third Jhāna, medium degree (18) Third Jhāna, minor degree
	3 Second Jhāna Planes		(17) Second Jhāna, highest degree (Ābhassarā) (16) Second Jhāna, medium degree (15) Second Jhāna, minor degree
	3 First Jhāna Planes		(14) First Jhāna, Mahā Brahmās (13) First Jhāna, Brahma's ministers (12) First Jhāna, Brahma's retinue
Eleven Planes of the Sensuous Realm	Seven Happy Sensuous Planes	Six Deva Planes	(11) Control others' creations (10) Rejoice in their own creations (9) Tusita — Delightful Plane (8) Yāma (7) Realm of the Thirty-three (Sakka) (6) Cātummahārājika – 4 Great Kings
			(5) Human Beings
		Four Lower Realms of Woe	(4) Ghosts (3) Asuras (2) Animal realm (1) Hell realms

And without fully comprehending these principles, there is no motivation to develop the detachment from the world that is essential to liberation.

Before examining the chart in detail, a few notes on terminology are in order. We will use the word "deva" to include *deva*, *devatā*, and *devaputta* referred to in the Suttas, as all three terms are almost synonymous. Although "deva" is often used in the Pāli texts to refer to all super-human beings, "deva" and "brahmā" can generally be distinguished. "Deva" in its more limited sense refers to beings in the six planes immediately above the human one (6–11), the sensuous heavens. When "deva" refers specifically to these sense-sphere beings, the term "brahmā" is used for those residing in the fine-material planes (12–27) and immaterial planes (28–31). If in a particular discourse "deva" is used for a being who clearly fits into the category of brahmās (as sometimes happens), we will call him a brahmā; if the deva is actually a sense-sphere being (or if his identity is unclear) we will retain "deva." For variety, we occasionally use "deity" and "god" as translations for *deva* in all its senses.

Let us now study some features of the chart. The lower beings and humans do not have fixed lifespans, but higher beings do. As you go up the chart from the sixth plane to the thirty-first, each successive group of deities lives longer than the group below it. The lifespans of devas are measured in multiple centuries. The duration of a brahmā's existence can only be expressed in aeons. The Buddha defines these extremely long periods of time by analogy. An aeon is the length of time it would take to wear away a mountain of solid rock six miles high and six miles wide, rubbing over it with a fine piece of muslin once every hundred years. The highest brahmās of the immaterial sphere live for 84,000 aeons.

All beings—human, sub-human, devas, and brahmās— die. All except Arahants are reborn in one or another of the thirty-one planes. No being lasts forever. Arahants have eradicated all mental defilements and have thereby eliminated the causes for rebirth with its attendant suffering. They are not reborn after death. Instead, they attain Parinibbāna, the complete, permanent cessation of every form of existence. For all non-Arahants, death is immediately followed by rebirth. The plane of birth is determined by the kamma that becomes operative at the moment of death. This could be any volition created in the present life or in any previous existence. Even the three lower kinds of noble ones (*ariya*) must be reborn. They have effaced some of the mental defilements, are assured of eventually attaining Nibbāna, and will never again be reborn in the lower planes. Noble ones of the two lower kinds—stream-enterers and once-returners—can be reborn in the deva planes. For anyone who is not an *ariya*—and this includes most devas and brahmās—the destination of rebirth is uncertain. It may be on the same plane or on a higher one; but most often it is on a lower plane. Rebirth is neither arbitrary nor controlled by a God. It takes place strictly due to kamma, the deeds we have performed and continue to perform all our lives. Brahmās too die and are reborn, and also suffer, even though their lives are so extremely long that they may be deluded into believing they are permanent.[1]

The devas of the sensuous sphere are said to enjoy sense pleasures in far greater abundance than can be found in the human world. Their bodies emit light and they have subtle sense organs, similar to ours but far more powerful and acute. That is why the supernormal powers of seeing various realms and hearing at great distances are referred to as deva vision and deva hearing. On the deva planes there are stream-enterers and once-returners. For example, Sakka, king of the gods in the heaven of the Thirty-three, became a stream-enterer while discussing the Dhamma with the Buddha, as we will see below.[2] However, only few among the devas have any understanding of the Dhamma. In fact, all that is needed to be reborn in these heavens is the meritorious kamma of generosity and good morality. Mental development through meditation is not a prerequisite for rebirth on the higher sensuous planes.

The fine-material brahmās have extremely subtle bodies of light; their powers aregreat but not unlimited. A being is reborn among these brahmās by cultivating the appropriate jhāna, perfecting it, and retaining it at the moment of death. Jhānas are states of deep concentration that can be attained by unifying the mind through meditation. They are all wholesome states of a very lofty and sublime nature. But one can get "stuck internally" in any of the jhānas and thereby block one's progress towards awakening.[3] There are four fine-material jhānas. The beings in the brahmā planes spend most of their time enjoying their respective jhānas. Brahmās experience no ill will or hatred, but only because they have suppressed it by their jhāna, not because they have uprooted it from their mental continuum. Thus when a brahmā is eventually reborn as a deva or human being he or she can again be beset by hatred. (After one birth as a deva or human, a former brahmā can even fall to one of the lower planes of the grossest suffering.) The brahmās also are prone to conceit and belief in a permanent self, as well as to attachment to the bliss of meditation. Fine-material brahmās can interact with the human plane if they so choose, but to appear to humans they must, like the devas, deliberately assume a grosser form.[4] Later we will meet a number of brahmās who converse with the Buddha.

The immaterial brahmās of the four highest planes have no material bodies whatsoever. They consist entirely of mind. They attained this kind of birth by achieving and maintaining the immaterial jhānas, four kinds of absorption taking non-material objects, and it is this kamma that became operative at their death. These brahmās can have no contact with the human or deva planes, for they have no physical bodies; thus we will rarely mention them. They spend count-less aeons in the perfect equanimity of meditation until their lifespan ends. Then they are reborn in the same plane, a higher immaterial plane, or as devas. After that they too can be re-born on any plane at all. So even existence without a body is not the way to permanently eliminate suffering.

Only practising the Noble Eightfold Path can bring suf-fering to an end. In fact, immaterial brahmās are in the un-fortunate position of being unable to start on the path. This is because one has to learn the Dhamma from the Buddha or one of his disciples to attain the first stage of awakening, to become a stream-enterer. That is why the sage Asita, called by the Buddha's father to examine the newborn Bodhisatta, wept after predicting that Prince Siddhattha would become a Buddha. The sage knew he was going to die before the prince attained Buddhahood. He had cultivated these imma-terial absorptions so he would have to be reborn in the im-material realm and would thereby lose all contact with the human plane. This meant he would not be able to escape saṁsāra under Gotama Buddha. He was sorely distressed to realize that he would miss this rare opportunity to gain deliverance and would have to remain in the round of re-birth until another Buddha appears in the remote future. He could see into the future and thus understood the precious opportunity a Buddha offers, but he could neither postpone his death nor avoid rebirth into the immaterial realm.

II

The Buddha Teaches Deities

The Buddha teaches deities when they visit the human plane where he normally resides,[5] and sometimes too by visiting them on the higher planes. On some occasions devas and brahmās come to the Buddha for clarification of Dhamma problems. On other occasions the Buddha becomes aware, through his supernormal knowledge, that a god needs some instruction to correct a wrong view or to goad him further on the path to awakening. Then the Buddha travels to the higher plane and gives the deity a personal discourse.

Once a brahmin admirer of the Buddha recounted as best as he could evidence of the greatness of the Buddha. He was trying to convince other brahmins to meet the Buddha. His proof included the fact that "many thousands of deities have gone for refuge for life to the recluse Gotama" (MN 95.9). Devas, like humans, develop faith in the Buddha by practising his teachings. In Chapter III we will see how grateful devas express this confidence. When devas come to visit the Buddha late at night, their luminous bodies light up the monastery as they pay respects to the Exalted One and ask their questions.

We will start with a god who was agitated by fear arisen from his sensual desire, and conclude with one who becomes a stream-enterer during his conversation with the Buddha.

Devas Come to the Buddha for Help

Subrahmā deva

Subrahmā deva was not a very sophisticated god; he delighted in sensuality, like many other devas of the sensuous sphere. He had been playing in sport with his thousand nymphs when half of them suddenly vanished. Subrahmā used his deva vision to find where they had gone and he saw that they had died and been reborn in a hell realm. Anxious that he and his remaining nymphs might soon suffer the same fate, he came to the Buddha looking for a way to end his fear:

> "Always frightened is this mind,
> The mind is always agitated
> About problems not yet arisen
> And about those that have appeared.
> If there exists release from fear,
> Being asked, please explain it to me."

The Buddha does not offer simplistic short-term solutions to the suffering beings go through when their loved ones die; he did not console the deva. Instead, he told Subrahmā that only by developing wholesome mental states through meditation and by giving up all attachments can anyone find security:

> "Not apart from enlightenment and austerity,
> Not apart from sense restraint,
> Not apart from relinquishing all,
> Do I see any safety for living beings."
>
> (KS I, 77; SN 2:17)

The deva and his remaining nymphs apparently comprehended these words, as the commentary says that at the end of this discourse they all became stream-enterers.

How to escape suffering

One deva who came to visit the Buddha seemed to be already trying to practise the Dhamma, for he was concerned about how beings can eliminate their internal and external bondage:

> "A tangle inside, a tangle outside,
> This generation is entangled in a tangle.
> I ask you this, O Gotama,
> Who can disentangle this tangle?"

The Buddha replied that to untie these knots of misery one must cultivate morality, mindfulness, concentration, and insight. He added that the Arahants are indeed freed from the twists and bonds of rebirth:

> "A man who is wise, established on virtue,
> Developing the mind and wisdom,
> A bhikkhu who is ardent and discerning:
> He can disentangle this tangle.
>
> Those in whom lust and hatred too
> Along with ignorance have been expunged,
> The arahants with taints destroyed:
> For them the tangle is disentangled."
>
> (KS I, 20; SN 1:23)

A second deva concerned with liberation spoke a verse which is partly praise of the Buddha and partly a request for teaching. Using various similes from the animal world, this god showed his admiration and reverence for the Exalted One. In the last line, with all humility, he posed the question that the Buddha's teachings are designed to answer:

> "Having approached you, we ask a question
> Of the slender hero with antelope-calves,

> Greedless, subsisting on little food,
> Wandering alone like a lion,
> An elephant indifferent to sensual pleasures:[6]
> How is one released from suffering?"

The Buddha treated this deva's serious query directly and with a minimum of words. He replied that the way out of suffering is to cultivate detachment from the eye, ear, nose, tongue, body, and mind:

> "There are five sensual cords in the world,
> Mind is declared to be the sixth.
> Having made desire fade out here,
> It is thus one is released from suffering."
>
> (KS I, 25; SN 1:30)

These two gods apparently had already prepared themselves for the Dhamma and did not need the kind of graduated discourse usually given to human beings, which begins with the benefits of generosity and ethics. We can contemplate and practise the Buddha's advice to the deities to cultivate the detachment and insight that lead to liberation.

Friendship with the good

Once a group of six devas came to visit the Buddha at Sāvatthī, while he was residing in Jetavana, the monastery offered by Anāthapindika. The first deva spoke the following verse:

> "One should associate only with the good,
> With the good one should foster intimacy.
> Having learnt the true Dhamma of the good,
> One becomes better, never worse."
>
> (KS I, 27; SN 1:31)

The other five concurred and spoke verses that differed only in their point of emphasis. One said association with the good brings wisdom, another that friends dry our tears, another that wise friendship brings one a good reputation, another that it leads to a happy rebirth. The last stated that a good friend is a source of bliss. The Buddha approved their verses and then added one of his own:

> "One should associate only with the good,
> With the good one should foster intimacy.
> Having learnt the true Dhamma of the good,
> One is released from all suffering."

Mahāmaṅgala Sutta

The popular Mahāmaṅgala Sutta—the Great Discourse on Blessings—originated when a radiant deva approached the Blessed One at Jetavana and respectfully requested a teaching on the highest good: "Many gods and men, wishing for well-being, have pondered over those things that constitute blessings. Tell us what is the highest blessing (*maṅgalam uttamaṁ*)." When gods cannot concur among themselves they go to the Fully Self-Awakened One, "the light of the triple world," the source of all wisdom. The Buddha enumerated thirty-eight "blessings," among them: rebirth in a good location, supporting one's parents, avoiding intoxicants, hearing the Dhamma, and knowing the Four Noble Truths (Sn vv. 258–69). This sutta to a deva is one of the select number of *parittas*, suttas recited for protection from harm, and is popular among Buddhists even to this day.

A discouraged meditator

A deva named Kāmada had been trying to follow the Buddha's teachings but found the task too demanding. He sounds depressed, as we human meditators feel when we cannot see any "progress" in our practice and lose sight of the long-term perspective. Discouraged, Kāmada complained to the Buddha about how difficult it is to practise the Dhamma.

The Buddha took a positive approach. He did not coddle or comfort the deva, but praised those bhikkhus who leave the household life to work steadfastly towards the goal:

> "They do even what is difficult to do,
> (O Kāmada," said the Blessed One),
> "The trainees who are composed in virtue,
> Steadfast are they in their hearts.
> For one who has entered the homeless life
> There comes contentment that brings happiness."

Kāmada remained disconsolate, insisting on the difficulties: "It is hard to win this serene contentment, Blessed One." The Buddha repeated that some beings do it, those "who love to achieve the mastery of the heart, whose minds both day and night, love to meditate." Meditation on the universal characteristics of change, unsatisfactoriness, and non-self is the way to ultimate contentment because it leads to detachment from all worldly concerns. Kāmada, however, complained that it is hard to compose the mind. The Buddha agreed the task is not easy, but added: "Yet that which is hard to compose, they do compose it" and, calming their restless minds, they attain the stages of awakening.

"The path is impassable and uneven, Blessed One," the deva complained. He seems to crave some magic to make everything easy. But that is not how the Buddhas teach: they only show the way, and we ourselves must put forth the energy to walk on. Liberation takes consistent, persistent, diligent effort. To Kāmada, not yet a noble one, training the mind seemed to be an endless task:

"Though the path is impassable and uneven,
The noble ones walk along it, Kāmada.
The ignoble fall down head first,
Straight down on the uneven path;
But the path of the noble ones is even,
For the noble are even amidst the uneven."

(KS I, 68–69; SN 2:6)

Would an Arahant say "I" or "mine"?

Other devas had more sophisticated queries. One deva, for example, asked the Buddha if an Arahant could use words that refer to a self:

"Consummate with taints destroyed,
One who bears his final body,
Would he still say 'I speak'?
And would he say 'They speak to me'?"

This deva realized that Arahantship means the end of rebirth and suffering by uprooting mental defilements; he knew that Arahants have no belief in any self or soul. But he was puzzled to hear monks reputed to be Arahants continuing to use such self-referential expressions.

The Buddha replied that an Arahant might say "I" always aware of the merely pragmatic value of common terms:

"Skilful, knowing the world's parlance,
He uses such terms as mere expressions."

The deva, trying to grasp the Buddha's meaning, asked whether an Arahant would use such expressions because he is still prone to conceit. The Buddha made it clear that the Arahant has no delusions about his true nature. He has uprooted all notions of self and removed all traces of pride and conceit:

"No knots exist for one with conceit cast off;
For him all knots of conceit are consumed.
When the wise one has transcended the conceived
He might still say 'I speak,'
And he might say 'They speak to me.'
Skilful, knowing the world's parlance,
He uses such terms as mere expressions."

(KS I, 21–22; SN 1:25)

Crossing the flood

Once late at night a deva came into the Buddha's presence, shedding bright light over the whole of Jetavana. He saluted the Lord, stood to one side, and asked: "How, dear sir, did you cross the flood?" This god knew that the Buddha had gone beyond saṁsāra's deluge of misery and wanted to learn how he had achieved this.

The Buddha replied: "By not standing still, friend, and by not struggling I crossed the flood." The deva, perplexed by this paradox, asked for clarification. To clear up the analogy, the Exalted One told him: "When I came to a standstill, friend, then I sank; but when I struggled, then I got swept away. It is in this way, friend, that by not standing still and by not struggling I crossed the flood." The metaphor describes balanced effort. He "sank" when he did not work hard enough, but if he strained too hard he became agitated and got "swept away." When he discerned how to cross over with just the right balance between energy and calm, he transcended the flood of suffering fully and permanently. This deva rejoiced that at long last he had met a real Arahant, a true holy man:

"After a long time at last I see
A brahmin who is fully quenched,
Who by not standing still, not struggling,
Has crossed attachment to the world."

(KS I, 2; SN 1:1)

The delighted deva had correctly perceived what set the Buddha apart from others: he had transcended death, rebirth, and all suffering by eliminating all the mental impurities. The deva began with a modicum of faith in the Buddha and received personal instruction from him. As a result, the commentary indicates, he became a stream-enterer. After the Buddha approved the deva's verse, he paid respects and departed.

Downfall

On a similar occasion a deva asked the Buddha to explain the causes of the downfall, or moral decline, of beings. In reply, the Buddha first gave a summary: "He who loves Dhamma progresses, he who hates it declines." Then he named ten specific dangers to avoid: (1) the company and teachings of the vicious, (2) excessive sleep and talk, (3) being irritable, (4) not supporting aged parents if one has the resources to do so, (5) lying to a monk or Dhamma teacher, (6) being stingy, (7) being conceited about birth, wealth, or community, (8) running around with many women, (9) drinking, gambling, and adultery, and (10) marrying a woman many years younger than oneself.

The Buddha concluded, "Reflecting thoroughly on those causes of downfall in the world, the wise one, endowed with insight, enjoys bliss in a happy state." Meditation on this negative subject makes wisdom grow, through avoidance, while encouraging insight and bringing pure happiness (Sn vv. 91–115).

Sakka's questions

Sakka, king of the devas in the heaven of the Thirty-three, played many roles in the Buddha's mission. He attended on the Bodhisatta at his final birth and at the Great Renunciation, visited the Buddha under the Bodhi Tree, and several times proclaimed his confidence in his unique qualities. A discourse called Sakka's Questions (DN 21) took place after he had been a serious disciple of the Buddha for some time. The sutta records a long audience he had with the Blessed One which culminated in his attainment of stream-entry. Their conversation is an excellent example of the Buddha as "teacher of devas," and shows all beings how to work for Nibbāna. For these reasons we will study Sakka's Questions in depth to see what message it has for us today.[7]

From his vantage point in the Tāvatiṁsa plane, Sakka was a keen observer of the behaviour of humans and other beings. He saw that while beings would like to live with each other peacefully, they rarely succeed. Thus his opening question to the Buddha attempted to unravel this contradiction:

> "By what fetters, sir, are beings bound—gods, humans, asuras, nāgas, gandhabbas, and whatever other kinds there may be—whereby, although they wish to live without hate, harming, hostility or malignity, and in peace, they yet live in hate, harming one another, hostile and malign?"

The Buddha explained that two mental factors—jealousy and avarice—cause all this trouble; from these two qualities almost all the aggression in the world arises. In this way the Buddha began a step-by-step lesson in Buddhist psychology: causes and conditions govern everything that happens in the universe. Sakka next asked about the origin of jealousy and avarice. Behind jealousy and avarice, the Buddha said, lie liking and disliking, and the source of both liking and disliking is desire.

As this is such a basic problem, Sakka wanted to understand the even more deeply the causes of desire. The Buddha told him that desire is triggered by thinking. Although he did not specify what sort of thinking, he must have been referring to unsystematic mental activity, the random thoughts in which the untrained mind indulges. When Sakka asked about the cause of thinking, the Buddha said it is the "tendency to mental proliferation." This is what brings about random thinking, which leads to desire, which in turn culminates in like and dislike. These in turn condition jealousy and avarice, from which arise the conflicts in our daily lives.

Sakka next shifted to a more directly practical issue: "How does one destroy this sequence that leads to so much misery?" He requested the Buddha to explain what should be done to eliminate this tendency to endless proliferation of mental activity. The Buddha replied that one should not blindly follow after every feeling that arises in the mind. Rather, meditators should pursue a feeling—whether it be a pleasant, painful, or neutral one—only if doing so contributes to the growth of wholesome qualities. If we are alert to our reactions and see that pursuing a feeling strengthens unwholesome tendencies, then we should relinquish that feeling. We will not get carried away by desire for more enjoyable feelings or by aversion towards pain and unhappiness.

Sakka once again was very appreciative of the Buddha's words and he next asked more specifically about the practice of bhikkhus. The deva knew that monks practise the Dhamma to the highest degree, in the purest form. As a god he could not become a monk, but he wanted to discover how monks acquire the restraint required by the monastic disciplinary code. The Buddha replied that the good bhikkhu pursues only bodily conduct, conversation, and goals which are conducive to the growth of wholesome qualities, to the attainment of Nibbāna. He rigorously restrains himself from everything detrimental to these aims.

Sakka had one more question about mind training: "How do bhikkhus control their senses?" Again the Buddha spoke of avoiding whatever leads to evil while cultivating the positive, this time referring to all kinds of objects—forms, sounds, odours, tastes, tactile objects, and ideas. This is a basic Dhamma theme: always avoid unwholesome actions while one works to create wholesome kamma.

Sakka wanted to take full advantage of his lengthy audience with the Blessed One, so he embarked on another series of queries. These deal with the variety of religious teachers he had seen in the world. Even a deva can be confused by the range of doctrines taught by "holy" people. He genuinely sought to learn: (1) if these teachers all taught the same thing, and (2) if they are all liberated. How often do we hear today, "All paths lead to the same goal," or "All spiritual teachings are the same beneath their superficial differences." But the Buddha, the Fully Self-Awakened One, replied negatively to both of Sakka's questions. He explained that spiritual teachers do not all teach the same thing because they have different perceptions of the truth. From this it logically follows that they cannot all be fully liberated.

Proclaiming where true liberation lies, the Buddha instructed Sakka that only those "who are liberated by the destruction of craving are fully proficient, freed from the bonds, perfect in the holy life." When evaluating spiritual teachers, bear in mind that liberation means destroying desire. Sakka approved of the Buddha's statement and remarked that passion pulls beings to repeated rebirth in happy or unhappy circumstances.

Sakka was so at ease with his Teacher that he then related a story which shows an unexpected aspect of deity-human relationships. Long ago he had gone to various human ascetics for advice on these matters with utterly unilluminating results. None of the yogis that Sakka had hoped to learn from had told him anything. In fact, as soon as they realized he was the king of the devas, one and all decided to become *his* disciples. Ironically, Sakka found himself in the awkward

position of having to tell *them* what little Dhamma *he* understood at the time. They had no teachings to give him.

Sakka had been delighted with this whole conversation.
He declared that it had given him a unique happiness and
satisfaction "conducive to dispassion, detachment, cessation,
peace, higher knowledge, enlightenment, Nibbāna." This was
the direction he had longed to travel, literally for ages. He
had at last made substantial progress with the guidance of
the Blessed One.

Inviting Sakka to delve further into his mental processes,
the Buddha then asked him what thoughts contribute to this
great satisfaction. In his final reply, Sakka declared he was
joyful because he foresaw six facts about his future: (1) As
king of the devas he had gained "fresh potency of life." (2)
At the end of this life, he would mindfully choose where to
be reborn, in a human or higher realm. (3) In that future life
too, he would follow the Buddha-Dhamma with wisdom,
clear comprehension, and mindfulness. (4) He might attain
Arahantship in that existence. (5) But if not, he would become a non-returner (*anāgāmī*) and, after dying there, be reborn in the highest Pure Abode. (6) Finally Sakka knew that
that existence would be his last; before it ended he would
become an Arahant.[8]

The king of the devas then spoke a verse in gratitude to
the Buddha:

> "I've seen the Buddha, and my doubts
> Are all dispelled, my fears are allayed,
> And now to the Enlightened One I pay
> Homage due, to him who's drawn the dart
> Of craving, to the Buddha, peerless Lord,
> Mighty hero, kinsman of the Sun!"

The sutta then indicates that Sakka gained the stainless
"vision of the Dhamma" by which he became a stream-

enterer. All his uncertainties about the path to final awakening had been dispelled by the Buddha's masterly replies to his questions, and his own past merits bore their proper fruit.

There is another discourse with Sakka as questioner (MN 37). It is set later on, at the monastery built by the woman lay devotee Visākhā for the Buddha in Sāvatthi. This time Sakka asked the Buddha: "How in brief is a bhikkhu liberated by the destruction of craving ... one who is foremost among gods and humans?"

In reply, the Buddha summarized the sequence that leads a bhikkhu to liberation:

> "A bhikkhu has heard that nothing is worth adhering to. When a bhikkhu has heard that nothing is worth adhering to, he directly knows everything ... he fully understands everything ... whatever feeling he feels, whether pleasant or painful or neither-painful-nor-pleasant, he abides contemplating impermanence in those feelings, contemplating fading away, contemplating cessation, contemplating relinquishment. Contemplating thus, he does not cling to anything in the world. When he does not cling he is not agitated ... he personally attains Nibbāna. He understands 'Birth is destroyed, the holy life has been lived, what had to be done has been done, there is no more coming to any state of being.' "

The cycle of dependent origination (*paṭicca-samuppāda*) explains that contact leads to feeling which in turn conditions craving, and craving causes clinging, which leads to rebirth and suffering. So by contemplating feeling and by seeing it as impermanent, unsatisfactory, and non-self, the bhikkhu gives up all craving and clinging. That is Nibbāna here and now. Delighted, Sakka paid respects to the Buddha and returned to the Tāvatiṁsa deva plane.

The Buddha Goes to Teach Deities

In several episodes the Buddha travels to higher planes to teach the beings dwelling there. While he generally visited the lower brahmā planes for this purpose, his most important course of instruction to the gods took place on the Tāvatimsa deva plane (No. 7 on the chart). The Pāli commentaries report that during the seventh rains retreat after his Enlightenment, the Buddha spent three months in the Tāvatimsa heaven teaching the entire Abhidhamma to his mother along with numerous other devas and brahmās. They had gathered there from the various deva planes of ten thousand world systems in order to listen to his exposition of this extremely precise philosophical psychology.[9]

Only higher beings could have remained sitting in a single posture this long, and continuity of attention is essential for properly grasping the Abhidhamma. "Infinite and immeasurable was the discourse, which went on ceaselessly for three months with the velocity of a waterfall" (Expos 19). But as the Buddha was a human being, his body required normal food. Thus everyday, in the terrestrial forenoon, he created an image of himself to continue preaching in Tāvatimsa, while in his natural body he came to earth to collect almsfood and partake of a meal. Venerable Sāriputta met him daily at the Anotatta Lake, and there the Buddha summarized for him what he had taught the deities the previous day. Sāriputta gradually passed all this material on to his own group of five hundred bhikkhu pupils, elaborating and organizing it to make it easier to comprehend.

The Buddha gave this profound teaching in a higher plane as it demanded super-human attentiveness. His chief student there was his mother, who had died a few day after his birth and was reborn in the Tusita deva-world. By teaching her the most subtle aspects of the Dhamma, the seven sections

of the Abhidhamma Piṭaka, the Buddha expressed his gratitude to his mother for having carried him in her womb and
bringing him into this world.

Mahā Brahmā

The stories of a Buddha going to teach a brahmā take place
on the plane of Mahā Brahmā, the third of the fine-material
planes (No. 14). Many people worship Mahā Brahmā as the
supreme and eternal creator God, but for the Buddha he is
merely a powerful deity still caught within the cycle of repeated existence. In point of fact, "Mahā Brahmā" is a role
or office filled by different individuals at different periods.

The Buddha has directly seen the origins of Mahā Brahmā
and understands what it requires to be reborn in his world.
In the Brahmājala Sutta (DN 1) the Buddha describes how a
supposed Creator God came to believe himself omnipotent
and how others came to rely on his sovereignty. His description was based, not on speculation or hearsay, but on his
own direct knowledge. The Buddha explains that when our
world system disintegrates, as it regularly does after extremely long periods of time, the lower sixteen planes are all
destroyed. Beings disappear from all planes below the seventeenth, the plane of the Ābhassara gods. Whatever beings
cannot be born on the seventeenth or a higher brahmā plane
then must take birth on the lower planes in other remote
world systems.

Eventually the world starts to re-form. Then a solitary being passes away from the Ābhassara plane and takes rebirth
on the plane of Mahā Brahmā. A palace created by his kamma
awaits him there: "There he dwells, mind-made, feeding on
rapture, self-luminous, moving through the air, abiding in
glory. And he continues thus for a long, long time." After
ages pass, he becomes lonely and longs for other beings to

join him. It just so happens that shortly after the brahmā starts craving for company, other beings from the Ābhassara plane, who have exhausted their lifespans there, pass away and are reborn in the palace of Brahmā, in companionship with him.

Because these beings seemed to arise in accordance with the first brahmā's wish, he becomes convinced that he is the almighty God: "I am the Great Brahmā, the Vanquisher ... the Lord, the Maker and Creator, the Supreme Being." The other brahmās, seeing that he was already present when they took birth in his world, accept his claim and revere him as their creator.

Eventually this misconception of a Creator God spreads to the human plane. One of the other brahmās passes away and is reborn here. He develops concentration and learns to recollect his previous life with Mahā Brahmā, but none of his lives before that. Recollecting that existence he recalls that Mahā Brahmā was considered the "father of all that are and are to be ... permanent, stable, eternal." As he is unable to remember further back, he believes this to be absolute truth and propounds a theistic doctrine of an omnipotent Creator God (Net 69–70, 155–66).

The Venerable Ledi Sayadaw, a highly renowned Myanmar scholar-monk of the first part of this century, gave a careful analysis of the powers of Mahā Brahmā in his *Niyāma Dīpanī* (MB pp. 138–39). He states that although Mahā Brahmā can perform all sorts of transformations, he cannot actually create independent creatures, change the kammic law of cause and effect, or keep anyone from growing old or dying. Brahmā can use his special powers to transport a man to the brahmā plane for a short visit, but he cannot ensure that someone will be reborn there.

Sikhin Buddha and Abhibhū

This story of a former Buddha's encounter with brahmās was recounted by Gotama Buddha to his disciples as follows. Buddha Sikhin took his chief disciple, Abhibhū, along on a visit to a brahmā world where he told him to give a discourse to the brahmā, his ministers, and his retinue.[10] Venerable Abhibhū then "instructed, enlightened, incited, and inspired" the audience with a talk on Dhamma. But the great brahmā and his cohorts did not appreciate what they heard. Instead of paying careful heed to the chief disciple's words, they felt insulted that a disciple should preach in the presence of the Master. In their pride, they considered themselves worthy of the direct attention of the Buddha himself. Sikhin of course knew the brahmās' unwholesome thoughts. Without addressing them directly, he urged Abhibhū to continue and "agitate them exceedingly" in order to force them to acknowledge that they were not all-powerful, permanent, or superior to this Arahant.

Abhibhū followed his master's instructions by working supernormal feats while continuing his discourse. Only rarely does a Buddha himself perform supernormal acts or permit one of his disciples to do so in the human plane. But in a brahmā world, where deeds that seem impossible to us are the norm, these tactics are appropriate. At times Abhibhū made his body invisible while speaking to the brahmās, at times half visible, at times fully visible. This masterful performance did humble those brahmās. They became more receptive, and realizing the monk was no ordinary human being, they exclaimed, "This is a marvellous thing: the great magic power and might of the recluse!"

Abhibhū then remarked to the Lord that while speaking in a normal voice in the Brahmā world, he could make the beings in the surrounding thousand realms hear what he said.

The Buddha, deeming this relevant to the occasion, urged him to show his prowess. By projecting and broadcasting his speech, the disciple strove further to stimulate a sense of urgency in the brahmās so they would realize the need to stop the cycle of birth and death. Although the lives of brahmās are full of the bliss of jhāna, they remain subject to continual subtle change, to death and rebirth, and to suffering. Abhibhū declaimed:

> "Arouse your energy, strive on!
> Exert yourself in the Buddha's Teaching.
> Sweep away the army of Death
> As an elephant does a hut of reeds.
>
> One who dwells diligently
> In this Dhamma and Discipline
> Will abandon the wandering on in birth
> And make an end to suffering."

Then Buddha Sikhin and his chief disciple left that brahmā realm. They had done everything they could to make the brahmās see their own limitations and encourage them to practise the Dhamma (KS I, 194–96; SN 6:14).

Baka Brahmā

A brahmā known as Baka once reflected privately that he and his plane of existence were everlasting. He thought that there could be no higher plane of rebirth and was convinced he had overcome suffering. The Buddha discerned his deep-seated wrong view and decided to pay him a visit. When he appeared in that brahmā world, Baka Brahmā welcomed him formally but immediately announced:

> "Now, good sir, this is permanent, this is everlasting, this is eternal, this is total, this is not subject to pass away;

for this neither is born nor ages nor dies nor passes away nor reappears, and beyond this there is no escape." (MN 49)

The Buddha, however, contradicted him, pointing out that every one of his claims was wrong. Just then Māra the Evil One joined the conversation. Māra's task is to prevent beings from being won over to the Dhamma, to keep them trapped in the cycle of birth and death, his own personal domain.[11]

Taking possession of one of the brahmā's attendants, Māra urged the Buddha, with a display of sympathy, to accept this brahmā as God, the creator of all beings. He told the Buddha that recluses of the past who delighted in things of this life and "who lauded Brahmā" won happy births afterwards, while those who rejected Brahmā had to endure terrible punishment. The Exalted One let him have his say and then called his number:

> "I know you, Evil One. Do not think: 'He does not know me.' You are Māra, Evil One, and the Brahmā and his assembly and the members of the assembly have all fallen into your hands, they have all fallen into your power. You, Evil One, think: 'This one too has fallen into my hands, he too has fallen into my power'; but I have not fallen into your hands, Evil One, I have not fallen into your power."

All beings subject to craving—humans, subhumans, devas, or brahmās—are said to be in Māra's power because they can all be moved by defilements and must drift along in the current of birth and death. But the Buddha and the Arahants have permanently and completely escaped Māra's ken and power, for they have eliminated all defilements. They have exhausted the fuel of rebirth and thus have vanquished the Lord of Death.

Baka Brahmā next speaks up on his own behalf. He reminds the Buddha of his opening statement on permanence. He warns him that it is futile to seek "an escape beyond" his own realm, then he cajoles and threatens him in the same breath: "If you will hold to earth ... beings ... gods ... you will be close to me, within my domain, for me to work my will upon and punish." The Buddha agrees that if he clung to earth (or any other aspect of existence) he would remain under the control of Mahā Brahmā (and Māra too), but he adds: "I understand your reach and your sway to extend thus: Baka the Brahmā has this much power, this much might, this much influence." The Buddha points out that beyond the thousandfold world system over which Baka reigns there are planes of existence of which he is totally unaware, and beyond all conditioned phenomena there is a reality that transcends even "the allness of the all"—a consciousness without manifestation, boundless, luminous on all sides—to which Baka has no access. Demonstrating his superiority in knowledge and power, the Buddha uses his psychic powers to humble Baka and his entire assembly. By the end of the discourse, these once haughty beings marvel at the might of the recluse Gotama: "Though living in a generation that delights in being ... he has extirpated being together with its root."[12]

A brahmā with wrong view

Once an unnamed brahmā gave rise to the deluded thought, "No recluse is powerful enough to reach my realm." The Buddha read his mind and proved him wrong by simply appearing before him and sitting at ease in the air above his head, while radiating flames from his body in a dramatic display of supernormal powers. Four great Arahant disciples—Mahāmoggallāna, Kassapa, Kappina, and Anuruddha—independently realized what had happened and decided to join their Master on this brahmā plane. Each disciple sat in the air respectfully below the Buddha—but above the brahmā—in one of the cardinal directions, shedding fire around himself.

A short dialogue in verse took place between Mahāmoggallāna, the Buddha's second chief disciple, and the brahmā:

> "Today, friend, do you still hold that view,
> The same view that you formerly held?
> Do you see a radiance
> Surpassing that in the Brahma-world?"

> "I no longer hold that view, dear sir,
> (I reject) the view I formerly held.
> Indeed I see a radiance
> Surpassing that in the Brahma-world?"
> Today how could I assert the view
> That I am permanent and eternal?"

According to the commentary to this story, the brahmā gave up his belief in his own superiority when he observed the magnificence of the Buddha and the Arahants. When the Buddha preached the Dhamma to him, he was established in the fruit of stream-entry and stopped thinking of himself as permanent. When this brahmā saw his own impermanence clearly and distinctly for himself, his former tenacious opinion that his world and life were immortal was uprooted. Many aeons of preparation, the brahmā's quick intellect, the Buddha's perfect timing, and the support of the four Arahants bore fruit in the deity becoming a stream-enterer.

After the Buddha and his Arahants left and returned to Jetavana, the great brahmā wanted to learn more about the powers of bhikkhus. He sent a member of his retinue to ask Mahāmoggallāna whether there are even more bhikkhus who can perform such feats. Moggallāna replied:

"Many are the disciples of the Buddha
Who are Arahants with taints destroyed,
Triple knowledge bearers with spiritual powers,
Skilled in the course of others' minds."

(KS I, 182–84; SN 6:5)

Not only do large numbers of bhikkhus have such special powers and the ability to know other people's minds, but there are numerous fully purified Arahant disciples of the Buddha as well. The emissary was glad to hear this answer, as was the brahmā when he received the report.

Mahā Brahmā knows his own limits

Once a bhikkhu with psychic powers visited the various celestial realms seeking an answer to the question, "Where do the great elements—earth, water, fire, and air—cease without remainder?" An exhaustive inquiry led him from one realm to the next, until he finally came to Mahā Brahmā. The first three times the monk asked his question, Brahmā replied evasively: "Monk, I am Brahmā, Great Brahmā, the Conqueror, the Unconquered, the All-seeing." Exasperated, the bhikkhu demanded a decent reply, "Friend, I did not ask if you are Brahmā … I asked you where the four great elements cease without remainder."

At this point Mahā Brahmā took the monk by the arm, led him aside, and told him, "The brahmās of my entourage believe there is nothing Mahā Brahmā does not see, there is nothing he does not know, there is nothing he is unaware of. That is why I did not speak in front of them." Admitting his ignorance, he advised the monk to return to his Master, the Awakened One, who rephrased the question and gave the appropriate answer.

In this discourse we have more evidence that a Buddha is far beyond Mahā Brahmā in power, teaching skill, and understanding, and much of the proof is volunteered by the Great Brahmā himself (DN 11.67–85).

Devas Learn as the Buddha Teaches Humans

We have observed devas and brahmās approach the Buddha and ask him questions and we have followed the Buddha on his journeys to fine-material planes to uproot the delusions of brahmās. The Buddha also instructs gods indirectly, when they overhear him teaching humans. In such situations, devas with the requisite supporting conditions from previous lives can attain awakening along with the human auditors. A number of suttas conclude with a statement that the discourse was applauded by many devas and brahmās who attained one or more of the stages of awakening while listening in. One example is a discourse the Buddha gave to his son Rāhula.

The Buddha had been instructing Rāhula gradually from the time he was ordained as a novice at seven years of age. The training became more profound as he grew in years and powers of discretion. By the time Rāhula was twenty-one, the Buddha decided it was time to lead him towards Arahantship. So one day, after the Blessed One had finished his meal, he told the young monk to come along with him to the Blind Men's Grove near Sāvatthi for the afternoon. Rāhula agreed and followed. But they were not alone, for the text tells us that "many thousands of deities followed the Blessed One, thinking: 'Today the Blessed One will lead the Venerable Rāhula further to the destruction of the taints.'" The commentary says that these gods had been companions of Rāhula's during a previous life in which he first made the aspiration to attain Arahantship as the son of a Buddha.

The Buddha sat down at the root of a tree and Rāhula also took a seat. The Buddha asked Rāhula if each sense organ, each sense object, each kind of sense consciousness, and each kind of contact is permanent or impermanent. Rāhula stated that they are all impermanent. We can deduce that the devas, invisibly present, were listening and simultaneously meditating on the appropriate answers. The Buddha asked: "Is what is impermanent pleasant or suffering?" Rāhula acknowledged that anything that is impermanent must be unsatisfactory or suffering. Then the Teacher queried: "Is what is impermanent, suffering, and subject to change fit to be regarded thus: 'This is mine, this I am, this is my self'?" "No" came the reply. The invisible audience too must have drawn the same conclusion.

Next the Buddha asked Rāhula if the feeling, perception, mental formations, and consciousness that arise through the contact of the six sense organs with their objects are permanent or not. These are the four mental aggregates that—along with material form—constitute a being. Rāhula again said that they are impermanent. He must have deduced that since the contact between the sense organs and their objects changes every instant, the aggregates that derive from them must also be transitory. And again he recognized that whatever is impermanent is unsatisfactory. He also understood that it is untenable to consider anything impermanent and unsatisfactory as "I, mine, or myself," as the concept of control is at the heart of our ideas of "I" and "mine."

The Buddha then concluded that once one understands these facts fully, and sees how all these things are causally connected, one becomes disenchanted with all conditioned things:

> "Being disenchanted, he becomes dispassionate. Through dispassion [his mind] is liberated. When it is liberated there comes the knowledge: 'It is liberated.' He understands: 'Birth is destroyed, the holy life has been lived,

what had to be done has been done, there is no more coming to any state of being.' "

That is, he attains full awakening, Arahantship, and is no longer subject to rebirth. As Rāhula listened to his father's words, his mind was released from the taints through non-clinging. By fully penetrating the discourse he had become an Arahant, fully liberated from suffering.

All the deva and brahmā spectators listening to the discourse attained the paths and fruits: "And in those many thousands of deities there arose the spotless immaculate vision of the Dhamma: 'All that is subject to arising is subject to cessation.' " Some of them, according to the commentary, became stream-enterers, some once-returners, some non-returners, and some Arahants. This variety was due to the differences in their prior preparation and present effort at the time of the sutta. Even though this discourse was geared to a young monk, while the Buddha spoke higher beings developed their own insight through hearing it and purified their minds (MN 147; also at SN iv, 105–107).

III

Devas and Brahmās Honour the Buddha

Everyone who has even glimpsed the magnificence of the Dhamma feels tremendous esteem for the Buddha. Deities realize that he had dedicated innumerable lifetimes to perfecting himself so that he could teach others the way beyond suffering. Because of their devotion to the Exalted One, devas gratefully come down to the human plane—though the earth is said to be repulsive to their refined senses[13]—to express their homage and affirm their devotion to the Supreme Teacher. This is the reciprocal aspect of the Buddha as "teacher of devas": his deva and brahmā disciples acknowledge their debt to their incomparable master. They venerate him for his extraordinary purity and unique capacity to train others. These Dhamma beneficiaries from the higher planes rejoice and offer profound homage to the Buddha because they see, over a broader temporal range than is perceptible to ordinary humans, how he offers beings the way out of the misery of saṁsāra.

We will look at several examples of how the gods paid respect to the Buddha, finishing with the Great Occasion. Not only do these incidents help illuminate the relationship between gods and the Buddha, but they can also serve as sustenance for our own *Buddhānussati*, meditation on the qualities of the Buddha. This kind of contemplation creates wholesome kamma by increasing our confidence in the Teacher and prepares the mind for deeper concentration and insight.

Sakka's praises reported by Pañcasikha

Once Pañcasikha, a celestial musician, messenger, and attendant on the deva planes, appeared before the Buddha. He reported that Sakka, king of the gods of the Thirty-three, especially honoured the following qualities of the Buddha and his teaching:

1. The Lord has striven out of compassion for beings, like no other teacher they can find.

2. The doctrine he teaches is "well proclaimed by the Blessed One, visible here and now, immediately effective, inviting inspection, onward leading, to be experienced by the wise for themselves."

3. He distinguishes and proclaims what is good and what is bad.

4. He explains the path to Nibbāna.

5. He has taught beings to become learners (i.e. stream-enterers, once-returners, and non-returners) and Arahants.

6. Gifts to the Buddha are well-given (because they bear great fruit) and are accepted by him without any conceit.

7. He practises what he teaches and teaches what he practises. There are absolutely no contradictions between his verbal and physical actions.

8. The Lord has gone beyond all doubt and accomplished his aim in regard to the goal and the supreme holy life.

Pañcasikha reported that when Sakka had said all this, the gods of the realm of the Thirty-three were delighted. Sakka then concluded by telling them to cultivate the wish: "May this Blessed Lord continue to live long ... free from sickness ..." as that would benefit devas and humans (DN 19.1–14). What Sakka recommends is a simple form of meditation on universal love. His audience must have been a group with mixed potential for Dhamma comprehension and he showed them a simple way to create wholesome mental kamma. Since they all agreed that the Buddha was a very great being, they were happy to listen to his praises from Sakka. This induced them to wish him good health so that he could teach more beings the way to Nibbāna.

Brahmā Sanaṅkumāra

Sakka is often shown leading his fellow devas in some Dhamma activity. Here he praises human beings who became noble ones and took rebirth on the plane of the Thirty-three, where they outshine the other gods in fame and splendour:

> "The gods of the Thirty-three rejoice, their leader too,
> Praising the Tathāgata, and Dhamma's truth,
> Seeing new-come devas, fair and glorious
> Who've lived the holy life, now well reborn.
> Outshining all the rest in fame and splendour,
> The mighty Sage's pupils singled out.
> Seeing this the Thirty-three rejoice, their leader too,
> Praising the Tathāgata, and Dhamma's truths."
>
> (DN 18.13)

For Sakka and his cohorts, the great renown and beauty of the new devas confirm the value of the Buddha's teachings. They are glad and therefore honour the Buddha and the Dhamma.

This verse comes at the beginning of a complex sutta which makes a number of interesting points about gods. Ven. Ānanda had asked the Buddha where many deceased disciples of the Magadha area had been reborn. Before answering, the Buddha directed his mind to find their plane of rebirth. While he was investigating in this way, a deva came to him and announced that he was the former King Bimbisāra, a stream-enterer. As a man, he had been a devoted lay disciple for many years and had now been reborn among the Four Great Kings (plane No.6). This deva related to the Buddha a long incident from the past that began with Sakka's remarks about newly arrived devas. The episode provided the answer to Ānanda's original question.

After Sakka finished speaking, the gods noticed that an unusually brilliant light shone on the assembly. Then its source, Brahmā Sanaṅkumāra, approached the gathering. The former Bimbisāra explained that whenever a brahmā descends to a deva plane he assumes a grosser form "because his natural appearance is not such as to be perceptible to their eyes." Brahmā Sanaṅkumāra then gave the devas a Dhamma talk in which he surveyed the central teachings of the Buddha. He began by praising the Blessed One's compassion:

> "Since the Lord, out of compassion for the world and for the benefit and happiness of the many, has acted to the advantage of devas and mankind, those ... who have taken refuge in the Buddha, the Dhamma, and the Sangha and have observed the moral precepts have, at death ... arisen in the company of ... devas."

Sanaṅkumāra concluded his discourse with words of great homage for the Buddha and the Dhamma. He said that if one were to praise the Dhamma as well proclaimed, etc., and then to add "Open are the doors of the Deathless!" one would be speaking in accordance with the highest truth (DN 18.27).

In the final portion of Brahmā Sanaṅkumāra's speech, he numbered the stream-enterers and once-returners who had recently been born in the deva planes. But he did not ven-

ture to comment on the number of worldlings who had ac-
quired merit:

> "But of that other race indeed
> Of those who partake of merit,
> My mind can make no reckoning,
> For fear that I should speak untruth."

Sanaṅkumāra appears in several other suttas, where he
always reveres the Buddha and the noble Sangha. One of his
stanzas, in which he extols the Buddha, is quoted several
times in the Pāli Canon:[14]

> "The noble clan is held to be
> The best of people as to lineage;
> But best of gods and humans is one
> Perfect in true knowledge and conduct."

(MN 53.25)

Bāhiya Dārucīriya

In the next story a brahmā intervenes to help a human
being receive the Dhamma. Bāhiya Dārucīriya was a non-
Buddhist ascetic. The brahmā, a non-returner (*anāgāmī*) from
the Pure Abodes,[15] had been one of Bāhiya's companions at
the time of the previous Buddha Kassapa,[16] when they were
members of a group of monks who had made a determined
effort to win Arahantship. Bāhiya had then failed in the attempt and was now reborn at the time of Gotama Buddha.

Bāhiya had lived as a recluse for many years and he was
respected by the multitude as a saint, even to such a degree
that Bāhiya himself almost came to believe this. But one day,
out of compassion for him, his old friend in the Pure Abodes
appeared to him in a visible body and shocked him out of
his complacency: "You, Bāhiya, are neither an Arahant nor
have you entered the path to Arahantship. You do not fol-

low the practice whereby you could be an Arahant or enter the path to Arahantship."

This had the desired effect, and Bāhiya begged his benefactor, "Then, in the world including the devas, *who are* Arahants or have entered the path to Arahantship?" His desire for release from the world was so sincere that he had the humility to admit his limitations and ask for a teacher to show him the true path to holiness.

The brahmā replied that a Buddha had arisen in the world and was living at Sāvatthī: "There the Lord now lives who is the Arahant, the Fully Enlightened One. That Lord, Bāhiya, is indeed an Arahant and he teaches the Dhamma for the realization of Arahantship." As a non-returner since the time of the previous Buddha, the brahmā knew precisely what Bāhiya needed and he spoke the succinct truth about Buddha Gotama and his teaching. Thanks to the intervention and the guidance of his lofty benefactor, Bāhiya Dārucīriya was directed to the Blessed One, whose brief and cryptic discourse had such a powerful impact that Bāhiya achieved Arahantship right on the spot (Ud 1.10, pp.18–19). After his death, the Buddha declared Bāhiya the foremost bhikkhu with respect to quickness of understanding.

A goddess honours the Buddha

Once a devatā, a goddess named Kokanadā, visited the Blessed One at Vesālī and recited verses in his praise:

> "I worship the Buddha, the best of beings,
> Dwelling in the woods at Vesālī
> Kokanadā I am—
> Kokanadā the daughter of Pajjunna.
>
> Earlier I had only heard that the Dhamma
> Has been realized by the One with Vision;

But now I know it as a witness
While the Sage, the Sublime One teaches.

Those ignorant folk who go about
Criticizing the noble Dhamma
Go to the terrible Roruva hell
And experience suffering for a long time.

But those who in the noble Dhamma
Are endowed with acceptance and inner peace,
When they discard the human body,
Will fill up the heavenly hosts of devas."

(KS I,40–41; SN 1:39)

Although this was apparently her first direct encounter with the Buddha, Kokanadā understood a great deal about kamma and rebirth. She saw that people are reborn in lower realms (including hell) because they lack insight and disparage the Dhamma. She also perceived that humans can attain deva or brahmā births by discerning the Four Noble Truths: suffering, its cause, its cessation, and the Noble Eightfold Path leading to its cessation. Her knowledge of Dhamma does not seem to go beyond this.

The Mahāsamaya Sutta

The Mahāsamaya Sutta, or Discourse on the Great Assembly,[17] is the most stunning illustration of higher beings coming to the human plane expressly to pay respects to the Buddha along with the Arahants. This "mighty gathering" took place when the Lord returned to the land of his ancestors, near Kapilavatthu. Five hundred recently ordained bhikkhus, from the Sakyan and Koliyan clans, came to him to declare their attainment of Arahantship. Devas from many thousands of world systems approached to observe the occasion.

Four brahmās from the Pure Abodes, noticing that most of the other devas had gathered in the Great Wood to see the Buddha and Arahants, decided to visit too. So they assumed grosser form, appeared before the Buddha, saluted him, and stood respectfully to one side. The first one announced why they had come:

> "Great is the assembly in the forest here, the devas
>   have met
> And we are here to see the unconquered Sangha."

Although "Sangha" can refer either to the community of monks or to all noble disciples, the adjective "unconquered" implies that the brahmās were admiring the Arahant monks led by the Buddha.

The second brahmā said:

> "The monks with concentrated minds are straight:
> They guard their senses as the driver does his reins."

The third used more similes to describe the achievement of Arahants:

> "Bars and barriers broken, the threshold-stone of lust
>   torn up,
> Unstained the spotless seers go, like well-trained
>   elephants."

The last one spoke these lines:

> "Who takes refuge in the Buddha, no downward path
>   will go:
> Having left the body he'll join the deva hosts."

(DN 20.3)

This brahmā knew that anyone who has genuine faith in the Buddha will not create kamma that could lead to a lower plane of existence. That is how taking refuge in the Buddha assures us of a deva birth, not some magical power of his.

The Buddha then told the monks that devas and brahmās from the surrounding world systems come frequently to see the Tathāgata and the Sangha. It is not Gotama the Sakyan prince that they honour, but Gotama the Buddha and the community of noble ones. The Buddha indicates that this is a general rule. Wise deities used to come to pay obeisance to past Buddhas and will do the same for future ones too.

Then, so the monks could learn their identities, the Buddha announced the names of the groups of devas and brahmās as they presented themselves before him. The list included earth-bound devas, the Four Great Kings with their retinues, asuras, Sakka, residents of the Tusita and Yāma planes, occupants of the sun and moon, denizens of the two highest deva planes, and Mahā Brahmā "shining bright with all his train." The Buddha related that the devas were saying:

> "He who's transcended birth, he for whom
> No obstacle remains, who's crossed the flood,
> Him cankerless, we'll see, the Mighty One,
> Traversing free without transgression, as
> It were the moon that passes through clouds."
>
> (DN 20.19)

This discourse illustrates another aspect of the relationship between the Buddha, the Supreme Teacher, and heavenly beings. Some of them only yearn for an audience so they can express their confidence in him, acclaiming him in public.

IV

The Role of Devas in the Buddha's Career

At pivotal moments in the Buddha's career, deities often played supporting roles. We read of devas showing respect at these turning points, helping him to overcome obstacles, and frequently proclaiming his feats far and wide.

The Bodhisatta's last birth

At the moment of the Bodhisatta's final conception the gods rejoiced. They knew that such a special being was arising after the long "darkness of ignorance" that set in when the Buddha Kassapa's Dispensation disappeared. After having perfected all the *pāramīs*, every Bodhisatta is born on the Tusita deva plane (No. 9) in his next to last existence. There he waits until all the requisite conditions on earth are ripe for the rekindling of the Dhamma. Then the Bodhisatta passes away and enters his mother's womb, and after ten months he is born. The attainment of Buddhahood requires a human existence with its characteristic combination of suffering and pleasure.

From the Venerable Ānanda, the Buddha's personal attendant, we learn about "the Tathāgata's wonderful and marvellous qualities," which he himself had heard directly from the Buddha:

> "Mindful and fully aware ... the Bodhisatta appeared in the Tusita deva plane ... Mindful and fully aware the

Bodhisatta remained in the Tusita deva plane ... for the whole of his lifespan.... When the Bodhisatta passed away from the Tusita deva plane and descended into his mother's womb, then a great immeasurable light surpassing the splendour of the gods appeared in the world with its gods, its Māras and its Brahmās, in this generation with its recluses and brahmins, with its princes and its people.... When the Bodhisatta had descended into his mother's womb, four young deities came to guard him at the four quarters so that no humans or non-humans or anyone at all could harm the Bodhisatta or his mother." (MN 123.7–8)

The conception of a Buddha-to-be in his final body causes unusual physical phenomena in various realms. In fact, certain natural laws govern the major events in the careers of all Buddhas, past, present, and future: "It is the rule, monks, that when a Bodhisatta descends from Tusita into his mother's womb," such a light appears and all these special phenomena occur (DN 14.1.17). The devas protect the Bodhisatta's foetus inside his mother so he can grow perfectly. They shelter the mother so she is at peace, free from sensual desire, and relaxed, enabling the baby to develop in ideal conditions.

The description of his final birth in this discourse shows how important the devas are to this unique baby. Queen Mahāmāyā gave birth standing under a tree in the woods near the village of Lumbinī:

"When the bodhisatta came forth from his mother's womb, first the gods received him, then human beings ... He did not touch the earth. The four young gods [the Four Great Kings of plane No. 6] received him and set him before his mother saying: 'Rejoice, O queen, a son of great power has been born to you.'... Then a great immeasurable light surpassing the splendour of the gods appeared in the world.... And this ten-thousandfold world system shook and quaked and trembled, and there too a great immeasurable light surpassing the splendour of the gods appeared." (MN 123.17–21)

The recluse Asita, who was associated with the court of the Bodhisatta's father, witnessed these heavenly celebrations. Asita was visiting the deva worlds at the time so he asked them, "Why are you all so happy and joyful?... I've never seen such excitement as this." The devas explained to him:

"In a village called Lumbinī, in the Sakyan country ... a bodhisatta has been born! A being set on Buddhahood has been born, a superlative being without comparison, a precious pearl of the health and goodness of the human world. That's why we're so glad, so excited, so pleased. Of all beings this one is perfect, this man is the pinnacle, the ultimate, the hero of beings! This is the man who, from the forest of the Masters, will set the wheel of Teaching turning—the roar of the lion, King of Beasts!" (Sn vv. 679–84)

Some of these devas were probably *ariyas* themselves, and others would have been aware of the infant's future destiny. They rejoiced that the way to the end of suffering would soon be expounded, and Asita, stirred by their revelation, went to see the new-born child with his own eyes.

Period of renunciation and asceticism

After living a refined life as a prince for many years, the Bodhisatta gradually became dissatisfied with this tedious round of hollow sense pleasures. His *pāramīs*, built up for aeons, came to the fore, ripe for the attainment of Buddhahood. He knew he had to find the way to release from suffering, so on the very night his wife gave birth to their only child he renounced the home life to become a recluse. Over the next six years he mastered the stages of concentration under various gurus and tormented his flesh with the most severe ascetic practices. Deities observed his progress from the deva planes and occasionally intervened. For example, when the Bodhisatta considered abstaining from all food, deities came and offered to infuse heavenly food through the pores of his skin, but the Bodhisatta refused:

> "Deities came to me and said: 'Good sir, do not practise entirely cutting off food. If you do so, we shall infuse heavenly food into the pores of your skin and you will live on that.' I considered, 'If I claim to be completely fasting while these deities infuse heavenly food ... and I live on that, then I shall be lying.' So I dismissed those deities saying, 'There is no need.'" (MN 36.27)

The gods, observing the Great Being, would not let him kill himself through voluntary starvation, but he on his part would not allow himself to speak untruth even by implication; thus he would not accept their offer. Although the Bodhisatta undertook long grueling fasts, he still did not come any closer to what he really sought: the way to uproot all the causes of suffering and so end rebirth once and for all.

Under the Bodhi Tree

After the Bodhisatta spent six years pursuing ascetic practices to their limit, he finally set out alone to discover another method to fulfil his aim. He had realized that self-torture was not the solution, so he started to consume normal food again. He walked to the place now known as Bodh Gaya in Bihar, India. There he began to meditate under a tree, using a method he recalled from a spontaneous childhood experience of meditation. He was determined either to attain full liberation then and there or else to die in the attempt.

According to tradition, as the Bodhisatta struggled against Māra beneath the Bodhi Tree, when Māra challenged his right to attain awakening, he asked the earth to witness how he had perfected himself for so long to reach Buddhahood. Many devas and brahmās joined the battle, vouching for his completed *pāramīs*. Thereupon Māra, along with his evil troops, was routed and fled the scene. This "calling the earth to witness" is memorialized in innumerable paintings and statues: the Bodhisatta, seated cross-legged in meditation posture, touches the ground by his knee with his right hand, a gesture intended to draw forth its testimony.

In the eighth week following the awakening, while the newly enlightened Buddha was still near the Bodhi Tree, he hesitated to teach the Dhamma, apprehensive that it would be too profound for human comprehension. Brahmā Sahampati then became aware of what was going on in the Buddha's mind. This brahmā, according to the commentaries, had become a non-returner under a previous Buddha and resided in one of the Pure Abodes. Distressed at the Buddha's hesitancy, he thought: "The world will be lost, utterly perish since the mind of the Tathāgata, Arahant, Supreme Buddha inclines to inaction and not towards preaching the Dhamma!" So he appeared before the Buddha, respectfully stooped with his right knee to the ground, paid homage and appealed to him to teach:

> "Let the Exalted One preach the Dhamma! There are beings with little dust in their eyes; they are wasting from not hearing the Dhamma. There will be those who will understand the Dhamma." (MN 26.20)

The Buddha then gazed out upon the world with his "eye of a Buddha," and having seen that there are beings "with little dust in their eyes" who would be capable of understanding the truth, he announced, "Open for them are the doors to the Deathless"—a gift that has come down to us through the centuries. Brahmā Sahampati was gratified and joyously thought, "Now I am one who has given an opening for the Buddha to teach the Dhamma to beings." The Brahmā then bowed to the Buddha and vanished.[18]

One might wonder why the Buddha, who had prepared himself for numerous lifetimes just to teach the Dhamma to other beings, needed the prompting of Brahmā Sahampati to set out on his mission. The commentary offers two explanations: (1) only after he had attained Buddhahood could the Buddha fully comprehend the actual scope of the defilements saturating the minds of beings and the profundity of the Dhamma; and (2) he wanted a brahmā to request him to teach so the numerous followers of Mahā Brahmā would be inclined to listen to the Dhamma.

Turning the Wheel of the Dhamma

Now that he was committed to transmit the Dhamma, the Lord had to find his first students. He determined that the five ascetics who had assisted him in his struggle for the last few years would be the appropriate auditors. Aware that the group was staying at Isipatana, a royal deer reserve not far from Vārāṇasi, he made his way there in stages. When the ascetics first caught sight of him in the distance, they decided not to greet him, for they believed he had reverted to a comfortable life and had abandoned the search for truth. However, as the Buddha approached, his unique demeanour dispelled this assumption and they listened keenly when he spoke. He taught them the Middle Way between the extremes of asceticism and immersion in sense pleasures, the path which he himself had followed when he abandoned futile austerities. The Buddha next explained the Four Noble Truths and the Noble Eightfold Path. While he spoke devas and brahmās paid close attention, and at the conclusion they sounded their applause upwards from the lowest plane of the earth-bound devas, through each of the six sense-sphere deva planes, even up through the Brahma-world:

> "The matchless Wheel of Dhamma, which cannot be stopped by any recluse, brahmin, deva, Māra, brahmā, or by anyone in the world, has been set in motion by the Blessed One in the Deer Park at Isipatana near Vārāṇasi." (KS V, 360; SN 56:11; also Vin. I,10)

Under the impact of this momentous event, the entire ten-thousandfold world system shook and reverberated, and a brilliant light appeared, far superior to that of all the devas and brahmās, matched only by wisdom illuminating the Truth. The gods were messengers conveying this wonderful news throughout the universe.

When the Buddha was ill

Devas came to the Buddha several times when he was physically unwell. Once the renegade monk Devadatta, who wanted to take over the Sangha by force, hurled a massive boulder at the Buddha. The stone splintered before it hit the Lord, but a small fragment lodged in his foot, causing severe pain. So for some time, the Buddha lay down "mindful and discerning," observing the painful sensations (KS I, 38–40; SN 1:38). Then a large group of devas came to see the Teacher, anxious for his welfare. Impressed by the perfect equanimity he displayed despite the wound, they spoke in turn, praising him as a bull elephant, a lion, a thoroughbred, a bull, an ox, for his ability to patiently endure painful bodily feelings— "racking, sharp, piercing, harrowing, disagreeable"—mindful and clearly comprehending, without becoming distressed.

A few months before the Parinibbāna, the Buddha spent the rains retreat near Vesālī, where he suffered from dysentery. According to the Dhammapada Commentary (to vv. 206–8) Sakka, king of the devas, found out the Blessed One was ill and came to nurse him. The Buddha told him not to bother as there were many monks to handle this task, but Sakka stayed on and looked after the Buddha's physical needs until he had recovered. Some monks were surprised to see the great deva doing such menial chores. The Buddha explained to them that Sakka was so devoted to the Tathāgata because he had gained stream-entry by learning the Dhamma from him (see above p.20). The Buddha then pointed out that it is always good to associate with the wise, to be in their presence and learn from the example of their actions as well as from their verbal teachings.

The Parinibbāna

Devas and brahmās were active at several phases of the Mahā Parinibbāna—the Buddha's final passing away at Kusinārā—as recorded in the Mahā Parinibbāna Suttanta (DN 16). This event was not just the demise of a greatly revered being but it also represented the personal consummation of his teachings. It was the utter, permanent cessation of the aggregates of the one who discovered and taught the way to the end of suffering.

A short while before the Buddha attained final Nibbāna, he lay down to rest between two sal-trees. They began flowering profusely, out of season. After some time, the Buddha told the monk who had been fanning him to go away. Then the Venerable Ānanda, his devoted attendant, asked him why he had dismissed that monk. The Buddha replied:

> "Ānanda, the devas from ten world-spheres have gathered to see the Tathāgata. For a distance of twelve yojanas

around the Mallas' sal-grove near Kusinārā there is not
a space you could touch with the point of a hair that is
not filled with mighty devas, and they are grumbling,
'We have come a long way to see the Tathāgata. It is rare
for a Tathāgata, a Fully Enlightened Buddha, to arise in
the world, and tonight in the last watch the Tathāgata
will attain final Nibbāna, and this mighty monk is standing in front of the Lord, preventing us from getting a
last glimpse of the Tathāgata!'" (DN 16.5.5)

The indomitable Ānanda, who had permission to ask the
Buddha any question, next wanted to know what kinds of
devas were around them. The Buddha said he saw lower
devas who are "weeping and tearing their hair" in distress,
moaning, "All too soon the Blessed Lord is passing away, all
too soon the Well-Farer is passing away, all too soon the Eye
of the World is disappearing!" But there were devas free from
craving who endured this patiently, saying. "All compounded
things are impermanent—what is the use of this?" (DN
16.5.6).[19]

After passing through the successive jhānas, the Buddha
finally expired, attaining Parinibbāna, the immutable cessation of rebirth. At that moment the earth quaked, as it does
whenever Buddhas pass away. Brahmā Sahampati, who had
entreated the Buddha to teach forty-five years earlier, spoke
a verse as a short eulogy:

> "All beings in the world, all bodies must break up:
> Even the Teacher, peerless in the human world,
> The mighty Lord and perfect Buddha has expired."

Sakka repeated a verse of the Buddha's on the theme of
impermanence.[20] While Sahampati used conventional speech
adoring the deceased Lord, Sakka spoke in impersonal and
universal terms. His verse makes an excellent theme for meditation and is often chanted at Buddhist funerals:

> "Impermanent are compounded things, prone to rise
>   and fall,
> Having risen, they're destroyed, their passing is truest
>   bliss." (DN 16.6.10)

All the "compounded things," which make up everyone and everything in all the world, come into being and perish. Only when they cease utterly never to rearise ("their passing") can there be the perfect bliss, Nibbāna. These stanzas by the renowned brahmā and the king of the devas show how the beings on the higher planes applied their insight into impermanence and suffering, even to the Parinibbāna of their Lord and Master.

After they had honoured the Buddha's body for a full week, the Mallas of Kusinārā decided it was time for the funeral. They began to prepare for the cremation but could not lift the body and carry it out the southern gate of the city. Puzzled, they asked the Venerable Anuruddha what was wrong. This great elder, renowned for his "divine eye," told the devotees that the devas had their own ideas of how to arrange the funeral. The deities, he said, planned first to pay "homage to the Lord's body with heavenly dance and song" and then take it in procession through the city of Kusinārā to the cremation site. The devas intended the cremation to be at the Mallas' shrine known as Makuṭa-Bandhana. The Mallas were happy to change their plans and proceeded unhindered to arrange the funeral as the devas wished. Out of respect the gods participated in all phases of the funerary proceedings. It is said that "even the sewers and rubbish-heaps of Kusinārā were covered knee-high with [celestial] coral tree flowers. And the devas as well as the Mallas ... honoured the Lord's body with divine and human dancing and song."

They transported the body to the Makuṭa-Bandhana shrine and placed it there. They wrapt it many times in layers of finest cloth, built the pyre of scented wood, and placed the bier bearing the Buddha's body on top. But when the men tried to light the fire it would not ignite. Again the reason lay with the devas. Anuruddha explained that the devas would not allow the pyre to be lit until the Venerable Mahā Kassapa arrived for the cremation. Once Mahā Kassapa and his group of bhikkhus had arrived and paid their last respects to the Exalted One's body, the pyre blazed up spontaneously, burning until almost nothing remained behind. (DN 16.6.22–23)

V

Liberation for Humans, Devas, and Brahmās

The encounter with suffering

Human beings, devas, and brahmās are the broad categories of beings in the "happy realms of existence." The human world is marked by a pervasive admixture of happiness and suffering. This dual nature is the main reason why Buddhas are born here. The uneven quality of human life enables us to realize the unreliable nature of happiness and inspires in us a sense of urgency about the need to win deliverance from suffering.

Unlike the beings in the lower planes, few humans are overwhelmed by unmitigated and excruciating pain. We do, of course, experience physical pain and mental stress, but such experience is generally intermittent. For the most part our suffering is of a more subtle character. We can observe that every pleasure brings along some measure of dissatisfaction. Our contentment is unsteady and secured with difficulty. We must struggle to satisfy our needs and desires, but become anxious the moment we succeed. Even when we are relatively happy we are beset by a deep, subtle kind of suffering. This suffering, which lies below the threshold of painful feeling, stems from the momentary vanishing of all the conditioned formations of body and mind. In spite of our pain, human beings with an inclination for the Dhamma can make the effort to live by the Five Precepts of morality. We can find the energy to train our minds towards the concentration and insight required for awakening.

In contrast, devas see far less of the evident kinds of misery in their daily existence. Some brahmās meet no gross suffering except when they look down at beings on lower planes. Many devas instantly obtain whatever sense object they wish for. Brahmās dwell in sublime bliss and equanimity. In the fine-material and immaterial spheres ill will is suppressed, and without it there is no mental unhappiness.

It is difficult for deities to appreciate that everything changes and to recognize that their present pleasure and bliss do not last forever. Like Baka Brahmā, many imagine that they are eternal. The subtler forms of suffering tend to escape them as well. Without help from a Buddha or one of his disciples, they do not understand that the impersonal conditions that will terminate their felicity are already in operation. Many of the higher beings, as we have seen, have no idea that they will die, that their worlds and lives are in flux, that they are not fully in control, but are decaying at every instant. So in spite of their excellent concentration and present opulence, they are even at a disadvantage compared to human beings, who are driven by pain and frustration to seek the path to deliverance.

How then can such beings be induced to meditate? Why should they become concerned with suffering and its cessation? We have indicated the answers to those questions in preceding chapters. This is the job of the Buddha as "teacher of the gods."

The devas aspire to be human

Some devas long to be reborn as human beings because they are aware of the greater possibility of comprehending impermanence, suffering, and non-self on the human plane.

There is no real illness on the deva planes. When a deva faces death, his aura begins to fade and dirt appears on his clothes for the first time. When the gods see these indications of impending death, they tell their friend:

> "Go from here, friend, to a good bourn. Having gone to a good bourn, gain that which is good to gain. Having gained that which is good to gain, become firmly established in it."

The Buddha then explained the devas' concept of a good birth and of what is "good to gain":

> "It is human existence, bhikkhus, that is reckoned by the devas to be a good bourn. When a human being acquires faith in the Dhamma-Vinaya taught by the Tathāgata, this is reckoned by the devas to be a gain that is good to gain. When faith is steadfast in him, firmly rooted, established and strong, not to be destroyed by any recluse or brahmin or deva or Māra or brahmā or by anyone else in the world, this is reckoned by the devas to be firmly established."

The last sentence refers to a stream-enterer. Only stream-enterers (and other noble ones) have such steadfast confidence in the Buddha, Dhamma, and Sangha. They will definitely attain final awakening and release, and until then will never be reborn on a plane below the human one. To become an *ariya* is the greatest achievement for any being lost in the round of rebirth. Only by entering the stream to awakening can beings proceed to eliminate all the causes of suffering.

The Buddha explained that the devas view a human existence as an excellent opportunity for growth in morality, giving, faith, and understanding. With compassionate concern for their dying cohort, they say:

"Go, friend, to a good bourn,
To the fellowship of humans.
On becoming human acquire faith
Unsurpassed in the true Dhamma.

That faith made steadfast,
Become rooted and standing firm,
Will be unshakeable for life
In the true Dhamma well proclaimed.

Having abandoned misconduct by body,
Misconduct by speech as well,
Misconduct by mind and whatever else
Is reckoned as a fault,
Having done much that is good
Both by body and by speech,
And done good with a mind
That is boundless and free from clinging,

With that merit as a basis
Made abundant by generosity,
You should establish other people
In the true Dhamma and the holy life.'" (It 83)

The devas urge their friend to become a morally upright human being. He should give up everything unwholesome, be generous, and, once established in faith and meritorious deeds, help spread the Buddha's message.

Not only do wise gods long for human birth to practise the Dhamma, they also rejoice when they observe people establishing themselves in the way to the cessation of suffering. Such deities are convinced that human beings like these are greater than themselves. In spite of all the magnificent sights, appealing perfumes and tastes, melodious music, and other sensual pleasures they have at their beck and call, these devas understand the unsatisfactory nature of existence sufficiently to value the effort to put an end to saṁsāric wandering.

In the sutta preceding the one quoted above, the Buddha spoke of "joyous utterances" devas give forth in three situations: (1) when a man is preparing to ordain as a bhikkhu; (2) when a person is "engaged in cultivating the ... requisites of enlightenment";[21] and (3) when someone attains the goal, utterly destroying the mental defilements. Whenever devas notice people engaged in the first two deeds, they rejoice saying, "A noble disciple is doing battle with Māra." When the devas see that someone on the human plane has become fully awakened, they declare: "A noble disciple has won the battle. He was in the forefront of the fight and now dwells victorious." They commend and extol the Arahant in verse (It 82).

Paths to awakening and happy births

The Buddha has explained in many ways that liberation is infinitely more valuable than any state of existence. Even blissful lives in the deva and brahmā planes invariably include subtle suffering, end in death, and are followed by uncertain rebirth. In a discourse called "Reappearance according to one's Aspiration," he said:

> "A bhikkhu possesses faith, virtue, learning, generosity, and wisdom. He thinks: 'Oh, that on the dissolution of the body, after death, I might reappear in the company of well-to-do nobles!' He fixes his mind on that [idea], establishes it, develops it. These aspirations and this abiding of his, thus developed and cultivated, lead to his reappearance there. This, bhikkhus, is the path ... that leads to reappearance there."

The Buddha repeated the same statement in regard to every happy plane as far as the highest realm of existence. The good kamma generated by positive mental qualities, conjoined with the aspiration for a particular birth, can bring about rebirth on that plane. So by cultivating these traits one can be reborn in any of the six deva planes. With the support of the requisite jhāna, one can take birth in any of the fine-material or immaterial planes. If, additionally, one has destroyed the five lower fetters and become a non-returner, one can be reborn spontaneously in the Pure Abodes.

The supreme aim, however, is Arahantship. If one has purified one's mind totally of greed, hate, and delusion, one would experience "the destruction of the taints." Hence the discourse culminates with a monk aspiring for Arahantship:

> "Oh, that by realizing for myself with direct knowledge, I might here and now enter upon and abide in the deliverance of mind and deliverance by wisdom that are taintless with the destruction of the taints!' And by realizing for himself with direct knowledge, he here and now enters upon and abides in the deliverance of mind and deliverance by wisdom that are taintless with the destruction of the taints. Bhikkhus, this bhikkhu does not reappear anywhere at all." (MN 120.37)

That bhikkhu's demise is parinibbāna, the end of all possible forms of suffering forever.

Although devas and brahmās have very long lives pervaded by inconceivable bliss, they are not inherently greater than human beings. As we have seen, they are all subject to repeated becoming. A deva may well be reborn on one of the lower planes. Brahmās can fall to a ghostly or hellish existence after one intermediate life as a deva or human. The Buddha states that even lives lasting many aeons in the highest formless planes can end in lower births.

Therefore such lives provide no security, but only temporary remission of the underlying disease, and if they are not dedicated to progress towards Nibbāna their value is virtually nil. One who has understood the noble Dhamma will look upon such modes of existence with revulsion and dispassion (see GS V, 41; AN X,29).

Only by becoming an *ariya* can one be sure that one faces no more lower rebirths and is headed for the complete cessation of saṃsāra. To become a stream-enterer requires three things. One has to (1) develop confidence in the Buddha, Dhamma, and Sangha, (2) relinquish any idea that rituals lead to liberation, and most important, (3) eliminate the deep-seated view "I am real and lasting" that characterizes all worldlings. By uprooting that deluded view, noble ones remove their tendency to create the heavy bad kamma that leads to birth in the realms of woe.

Sometimes lay people, not yet ripe enough to desire liberation, asked the Buddha how to be successful in their mundane endeavours or how to be reborn on a celestial plane after death. The Master would reply with a discourse suited to their limited ability and inclination. He would tell them to give generously and live a moral life. He would specifically urge them to observe the Five Precepts without a breach and to undertake the Eight Precepts on special occasions. Generating such good kamma is the way to general well-being, now and after death. These basic steps form the starting point of the gradual training that leads all the way to Arahantship. The Dhamma is consistent from start to finish.

When the Buddha describes the entire course of a bhikkhu's training, from leaving home to Arahantship, he devotes considerable attention to the jhānas, the highest form of concentration. One who can keep the mind absorbed on a single object can apply this capacity for attention to insight, the wisdom section of the path. One skilled in jhāna can easily discern the impermanence, unsatisfactoriness, and selfless nature of the aggregates for extended periods. The jhānas

also create strong wholesome kamma, as they are all associated with some form of wisdom.

Individuals who practise the jhānas but do not reflect on
them with insight may think the jhānas permanently efface
their unwholesome tendencies. The Buddha found, however,
that mental defilements are only suppressed—perhaps for a
very long time—by these meditative states. Such absorptions
bring bliss and peace here and now, generate wholesome
kamma, and may bring rebirth in a plane of the brahmā world.
However, they do not uproot the latent defilements and thus
cannot cut off the root causes of saṁsāra. For this one needs
insight-wisdom, the discernment of the three universal marks
of impermanence, suffering, and non-self.

Conclusion

Let us human beings apply ourselves wholeheartedly and
take up the unique opportunity given by our present birth.
In the round of saṁsāra it is extremely rare to rise above the
realms of woe, where the way out of suffering cannot be
followed, and a human birth is even more favourable to awakening than birth in the realm of the gods. Devas envy us our
place, ostensibly so low on the cosmic scale, and wish to be
reborn as humans. The Buddha Sāsana still thrives, the
Dhamma is available in full, there are excellent teachers who
are true disciples of the Master, and we are on the best plane
for striving.

Final awakening does not bring "eternal life" in some
heaven as many religions promise. Nibbāna means letting
go of everything—relinquishing every state of being anywhere
in the cosmos. It is our attachments and cravings, rooted in
ignorance, that keep us revolving in saṁsāra's misery. Wisdom shows how all existence is bound up with suffering and
thereby illuminates the futility of all craving for being. Then

all old kamma is burnt up and no new fuel for birth is created. The process of birth and death just stops, once and for all. This is not the end of an existing being, as no such being ever was. It is only the end of a process, of the flux of physical and mental phenomena arising and vanishing due to complex networks of causes and conditions. There is no controlling or enduring self of any sort at any time.

What the Buddha taught deities, he taught people; what he taught people, he taught devas and brahmās: just the universal fact of suffering, and the way to the cessation of suffering—morality, concentration, and wisdom.

For the Welfare of Many

> The teacher, the great sage,
> Is the first in the world;
> Following him is the disciple
> Whose composure is perfected;
> And then the learner training
> On the path, one who has
> Learned much and is virtuous.
>
> These three are chief
> Amongst devas and humans:
> Illuminators, preaching Dhamma,
> Opening the door to the Deathless,
> They free many people from bondage.
>
> Those who follow the path
> Well taught by the unsurpassed
> Caravan-leader, who are diligent
> In the Sublime One's dispensation,
> Make an end of suffering
> Within this very life itself.

(It 84)

Notes

In some cases my quotations from existing translations have been modified, especially when quoting from GS. Quotations from MLDB invariably, and from Ud, It, and LDB usually, are exactly as they occur in these contemporary translations. Bhikkhu Bodhi's draft translation of SN is quoted verbatim.

1. Only *ariyas*, noble ones, can be sure that they will never suffer the agony of rebirth in one of the lower realms where suffering is incredibly intense and all-pervasive.

2. It seems probable that some devas become anāgāmis or even Arahants while practising the Buddha's teachings in the celestial planes, but I cannot cite any canonical texts to support this.

3. This phrase comes from Ven. Mahākaccāna's elucidation of a brief remark by the Buddha: "And how, friends, is the mind called 'stuck internally'? Here, quite secluded from sensual pleasures, secluded from unwholesome states, a bhikkhu enters upon and abides in the first jhāna, which is accompanied by applied and sustained thought, with rapture and pleasure born of seclusion. If his consciousness follows after the rapture and pleasure born of seclusion, then his mind is called 'stuck internally.' ... If his consciousness does not follow after the rapture and pleasure born of seclusion ... then his mind is called 'not stuck internally' " (MN 138.12). Clinging to a jhāna one has attained can prevent one from attaining awakening.

4. This phenomena is mentioned several times. Once, for example, a bhikkhu named Hatthaka had become an anāgāmi. When he died, he was reborn in the Aviha brahmā plane, the lowest of the Pure Abodes. Shortly after arising there he came to see

the Buddha. Hatthaka intended to stand "in the presence of the Exalted One," yet he was "unable to do so, but sunk down, collapsed, could not stand upright." Seeing this, the Buddha told him, "Create a gross body form." Once he had done so, he could stand at one side and have a discussion with the Buddha (GS I, 257; AN III, 125).

5. The opening section of the Saṁyutta Nikāya is devoted entirely to dialogues between the Buddha and various gods.

6. The Pāli word *nāga* is used to refer to any powerful creature, particularly the cobra and the bull elephant. In relation to the Buddha and the Arahants it is used in this latter sense; see Dhp. Nāgavagga (Chap. 23).

7. Direct quotations from the sutta are from the Walshe translation unless otherwise noted. See Bibliography for details of all translations consulted for this discourse.

8. This paragaraph is based on Sister Vajirā's translation.

9. The commentary points out that the Buddha himself first penetrated the Abhidhamma during the fourth of the seven weeks he spent meditating near the Bodhi Tree immediately following his awakening (Expos 16–17).

10. We may deduce that they proceeded to the third plane of the first jhāna, No. 14. The brahmā must have been the incumbent Mahā Brahmā, the God All-Mighty of many religions. That would make his ministers and retinue the occupants of the two brahmā planes lower than Mahā Brahmā's own realm, Nos. 13 and 12 respectively.

11. That the being Māra is a deva on the highest deva plane accentuates the fact that the gods are not necessarily wise or good. Māra also stands for death and defilements.

12. The part of the discourse about the brahmās ends here, but Māra was unhappy with this turn of events and interceded again, urging the Buddha not to share what he had learned with others. See MLDB for the complete sutta (No. 49).

13. The Arahant Kumāra Kassapa once said, "Human beings are generally considered unclean, evil-smelling, horrible, revolting by the devas," so they rarely visit this world. See DN 23.9.

14. For example by Ānanda at MN 53.25; by the Buddha at DN 3.1.28.

15. The Pure Abodes are the highest fine-material brahmā planes (Nos. 23–27) and are populated exclusively by anāgāmis and Arahants. The anāgāmis will never be reborn on a plane below the Pure Abodes because they have eliminated all traces of ill will and desire for sense pleasures. When they have become Arahants in the Pure Abodes, they will, of course, have no more births anywhere at all.

16. The same brahmā helped another member of that group attain Arahantship under Buddha Gotama. The brahmā gave a detailed riddle to Kumāra Kassapa and told him to ask the Buddha its meaning. When the bhikkhu received the explanation of the imagery, he attained Arahantship. See MN 23.

17. DN 20. See also Sayagyi U Chit Tin, *The Great Occasion*.

18. This story appears at MN 26.19–21; SN 6:1 (= KS I, 171–74); also at Vin. I, 4–7.

19. "Devas who are free from craving" refers to brahmās from the Pure Abodes.

20. See LDB 290, DN 17.2.17.

21. These are the thirty-seven *bodhipakkhiyā dhammā*, such as the four foundations of mindfulness, etc. See DN 16.3.50.

Abbreviations

AN   Aṅguttara Nikāya

DN   Dīgha Nikāya

Dial   Dialogues of the Buddha (Dīgha Nikāya)

Expos   Expositor (trans. of Atthasālinī)

GS   Gradual Sayings (trans. of Aṅguttara Nikāya)

It   Itivuttaka

KS   Kindred Sayings (trans. of Saṃyutta Nikāya)

LDB   Long Discourses of the Buddha (trans. of Dīgha Nikāya)

MN   Majjhima Nikāya

MB   Manuals of Buddhism

MLDB   Middle Length Discourses of the Buddha (trans. of Majjhima Nikāya)

MLS   Middle Length Sayings (trans. of Majjhima Nikāya)

Net   Net of Views (Brahmājala Sutta)

SN   Saṃyutta Nikāya

Sn   Sutta-nipāta

Vin   Vinaya Piṭaka

Bibliography

References to MN and DN are by sutta and section number of MLDB and LDB respectively; to SN (and its translation KS), by chapter and sutta number, with page numbers of KS; to AN (and its translation GS), by nipāta and sutta number, with page numbers of GS; to the Udāna, by chapter and section; to It, by sutta number. Verses ofSN are from a draft translation by Bhikkhu Bodhi (in progress).

PALI TEXT SOCIETY

* Kindred Sayings
* Gradual Sayings
* Middle Length Sayings
* The Group of Discourses
* Dialogues of the Buddha
* The Expositor

BUDDHIST PUBLICATION SOCIETY

* Udāna, trans. John D. Ireland, 1990
* The Itivuttaka, trans. John D. Ireland, 1991
* The Dhammapada, trans. Acharya Buddharakkhita, 1985
* The All-Embracing Net of Views (Brahmajāla Sutta), trans. Bhikkhu Bodhi, 1978
* Sakka's Quest, trans. Sister Vajirā (Wheel No. 10)

WISDOM PUBLICATIONS

* Long Discourses of the Buddha, trans. Maurice Walshe. 1987, 1995
* Middle Length Discourses of the Buddha, trans. Bnikkhu Ñāṇamoli & Bhikkhu Bodhi, 1995

OTHER

* The Sutta-Nipāta, trans. H. Saddhatissa. London: Curzon, 1985
* Manuals of Buddhism, Ledi Sayadaw. Rangoon, 1981
* The Great Occasion, Sayagyi U Chit Tin. Sayagyi U Ba Khin Memorial Trust, U.K.

THE BUDDHIST PUBLICATION SOCIETY

The BPS is an approved charity dedicated to making known the Teaching of the Buddha, which has a vital message for people of all creeds. Founded in 1958, the BPS has published a wide variety of books and booklets covering a great range of topics. Its publications include accurate annotated translations of the Buddha's discourses, standard reference works, as well as original contemporary expositions of Buddhist thought and practice. These works present Buddhism as it truly is—a dynamic force which has influenced receptive minds for the past 2500 years and is still as relevant today as it was when it first arose. A full list of our publications will be sent upon request. Write to:

The Hony. Secretary
BUDDHIST PUBLICATION SOCIETY
P.O. Box 61
54, Sangharaja Mawatha
Kandy • Sri Lanka